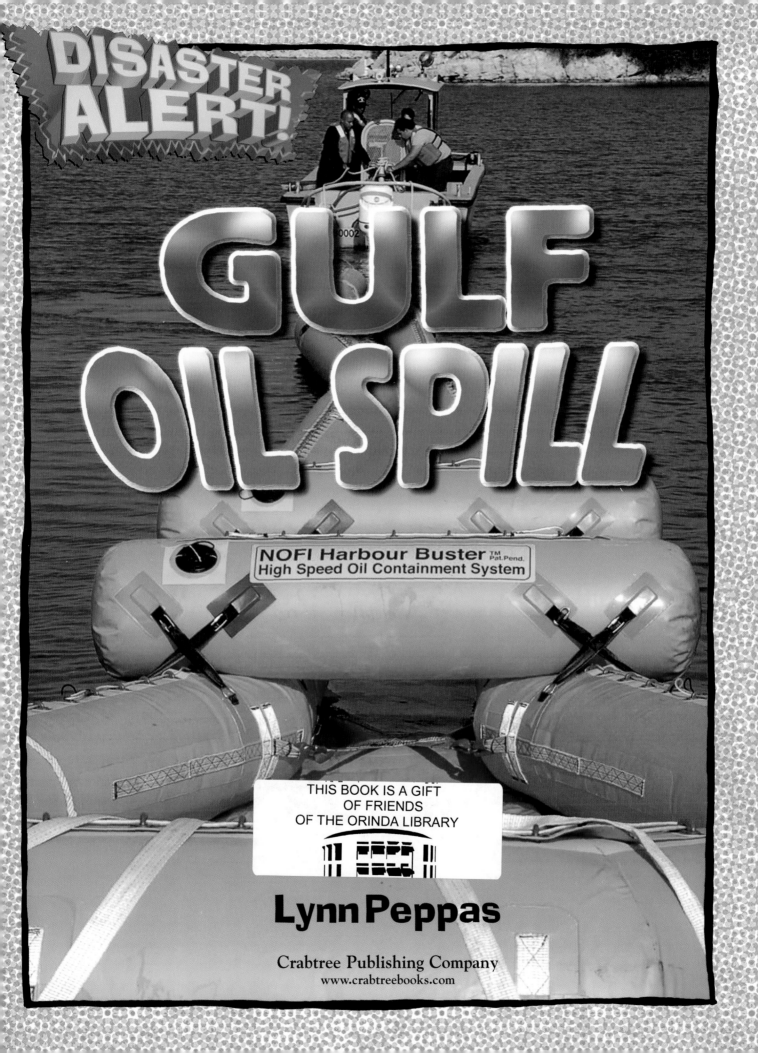

DISASTER ALERT!

GULF OIL SPILL

NOFI Harbour Buster™ Pat.Pend.
High Speed Oil Containment System

Lynn Peppas

Crabtree Publishing Company
www.crabtreebooks.com

Crabtree Publishing Company

www.crabtreebooks.com

Project editor: Paul Challen

Project coordinator: Kathy Middleton

Editor: Adrianna Morganelli

Proofreaders: Rachel Stuckey, Crystal Sikkens

Book design: Tibor Choleva

Cover design: Ken Wright

Photo research: Tibor Choleva, Melissa McClellan

Prepress technician: Margaret Amy Salter

Print and production coordinator: Katherine Berti

Consultant: Hugh S. Gorman

Photographs: U.S. Defense Imagery: U.S. Navy photo byPaul Farley (title page); U.S. Coast Guard photos by Petty Officer 3rd Class Patrick Kelley (table of contents page, page 23 bottom); U.S. Air Force photo by Tech. Sgt. Adrian Cadiz (page 13); U.S. Navy photo by Journalist 2nd Class Steve Vasquez (page 17 top); U.S. Air Force photo by Senior Airman Bryan Nealy (page 17 bottom); U.S. Coast Guard photos by Petty Officer 3rd Class Ann Marie Gorden (pages 18, 20, 29 bottom); U.S. Coast Guard photo by Public Affairs Specialist 3rd Class Colin White (page 21 top); U.S. Coast Guard photo by Petty Officer 2nd Class Gary Rives (page 21 bottom); U.S. Coast Guard photo by Petty Officer 1st Class John Masson (page 22); U.S. Navy photo by Mass Communication Specialist 2nd Class Jonathen E. Davis (page 23 top); U.S. Coast Guard photo by Petty Officer 3rd Class Robert Brazzell (page 26); U.S. Navy photo by Mass Communication Specialist 2nd Class Justin Stumberg (page 27 top); U.S. Navy photo by Mass Communication Specialist 2nd Class

David Didier (page 30); U.S. Air Force photo by Senior Airman Bryan Nealy (page 31); U.S. Coast Guard photo by Richard Brahm (cover)

NASA: page 16

© NOAA: page 5, page 24; page 25 top; page 27 bottom

© BP p.l.c. (page 19 top)

Dreamstime.com: © Leofrancini (page 9 top)

Shutterstock.com: © AridOcean (page 6); © Ingvar Tjostheim (pages 9 bottom, 10 right, 11 top and bottom,15); © Ljupco Smokovski (page 14–15 red flags); © Andrey Armyagov (page 25 middle); Rich Carey (page 25 bottom); © Lucarelli Temistocle (page 28); © Danny E Hooks (page 29 top)

AP images: © AP/ Charlie Riedel (page 4); © AP/ Gerald Herbert (page 12)

© Xinhua/Xinhua Press/Corbis (page 14)

Illustrations: David Brock: p. 7, 8, 10; Tibor Choleva: p 19

Cover: Crews battle the fire on the Deepwater Horizon oil rig after the disastrous blowout.

Title page: Harbour Buster high speed oil containment system is towed by a U.S. Navy boat.

Contents: A worker cleans up oily waste on Elmer's Island just west of Grand Isle, LA., May 21, 2010.

Every attempt has been made to clear copyright. Should there be any inadvertent omission, a correction will be made in a subsequent reprint.

This book was produced for Crabtree Publishing Company by SilverDot Publishing.

Library and Archives Canada Cataloguing in Publication

Peppas, Lynn
   Gulf oil spill / Lynn Peppas.

(Disaster alert!)
Includes index.
Issued also in electronic format.
ISBN 978-0-7787-1592-4 (bound).--ISBN 978-0-7787-1625-9 (pbk.)

   1. BP Deepwater Horizon Explosion and Oil Spill, 2010--Juvenile literature. 2. Oil spills--Mexico, Gulf of--Juvenile literature.
I. Title. II. Series: Disaster alert!

GC1221.P46 2011   j363.11'9622338190916364   C2011-901619-2

Library of Congress Cataloging-in-Publication Data

Peppas, Lynn.
   Gulf oil spill / Lynn Peppas.
      p. cm. -- (Disaster alert!)
   Includes index.
   ISBN 978-0-7787-1592-4 (reinforced library binding : alk. paper) --
ISBN 978-0-7787-1625-9 (pbk. : alk. paper) -- ISBN 978-1-4271-9620-0
(electronic (pdf))
   1. BP Deepwater Horizon Explosion and Oil Spill, 2010--Juvenile literature. 2.
Oil spills--Mexico, Gulf of--Juvenile literature. I. Title.
   GC1221.B46 2011
   363.11'9622338190916364--dc22
                                                     2011008787

Printed in Canada/042011/KR20110304

Published in Canada
Crabtree Publishing
616 Welland Ave.
St. Catharines, Ontario
L2M 5V6

Published in the United States
Crabtree Publishing
PMB 59051
350 Fifth Avenue, 59th Floor
New York, New York 10118

Published in the United Kingdom
Crabtree Publishing
Maritime House
Basin Road North, Hove
BN41 1WR

Published in Australia
Crabtree Publishing
386 Mt. Alexander Rd.
Ascot Vale (Melbourne)
VIC 3032

Table of Contents

Disaster on the Water

The Gulf Oil Spill is one of the largest **marine** oil spills in history. In 2010, it was the largest oil spill to ever happen in water. The disastrous **blowout** happened on the Deepwater Horizon oil rig in the Gulf of Mexico on April 20, 2010. A number of workers on the oil rig were killed and millions of gallons of oil poured into the ocean for months before the massive leak was stopped.

What is a disaster?
A disaster is a destructive event that affects the natural world and human communities. Some disasters are predictable and others occur without warning. Coping successfully with a disaster often depends on a community's preparation.

Marine birds such as brown pelicans make the Gulf of Mexico their home. Many were harmed by the oil that reached the shores.

Deepwater Horizon

The Deepwater Horizon oil rig was drilling an oil well at the Macondo Prospect in the Gulf of Mexico when a blowout occurred. A blowout is a burst of oil and gas under high pressure that moves upward from an oil well to the rig. Oil and gas caught on fire and burned the oil rig. Many workers escaped on lifeboats. Eleven workers died in the explosion.

Other Disastrous Oil Spills

The Gulf Oil Spill was not the first disastrous oil spill to ever happen. Oil spills occur on land or in water, all around the world. Accidents do not happen often, but when they do, they can be disastrous for people, animals, and the environment.

Another offshore rig accident happened in the Gulf of Mexico in 1979. While drilling an underwater well, a rig called Ixtoc 1 suffered a blowout. Even though it is one of the largest oil spills in history it did not release as much oil as the 2010 Gulf Oil Spill.

Smaller oil spills happen when ships that transport oil, called oil tankers, have accidents on the water. In 1989, an oil tanker called the Exxon Valdez ran into a reef offshore from the U.S. state of Alaska. Hundreds of thousands of barrels of oil were spilled into the ocean.

Oil spills cause a lot of damage to wildlife and the environment.

Underwater Oil

People depend on oil for energy. Oil powers vehicles, factories, and heats or cools homes. It is also used to create products such as plastics, medicines, and clothing. The United States uses more oil than any other country on Earth—almost 20 million barrels of oil every day. Almost one third of all U.S. **domestic** oil comes from thousands of offshore wells in the Gulf of Mexico, such as the one at the Macondo Prospect site.

Macondo Prospect is located approximately 50 miles (80.5 km) southwest of the Mississippi River Delta at the edge of the continental shelf.

USA

New Orleans

Tampa

Miami

Houston

Austin

GULF OF MEXICO

CUBA

MEXICO

The Gulf of Mexico

The Gulf of Mexico is a large, saltwater basin that is partially surrounded by the United States, Mexico, and Cuba. It is believed to be over 300 million years old. A continental shelf stretches under water from the shoreline of these landmasses. The ocean water that covers the continental shelf is shallow. At its deepest point, the water is less than 1,000 feet (305 m) deep. The continental slope drops off from the shelf to depths of up to 5,000 feet (1,524 m). The slope has hills and valleys that resemble land features but are under water.

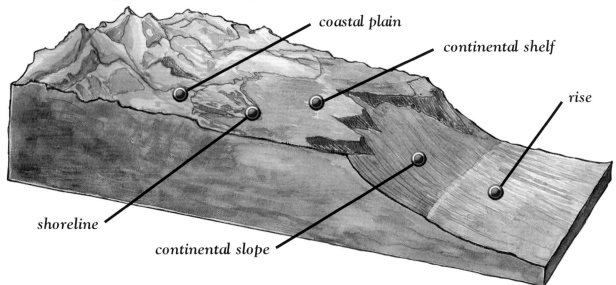

coastal plain

continental shelf

rise

shoreline

continental slope

Crude Oil

Crude oil is sometimes called petroleum. Scientists believe it is the product of ancient living organisms such as plants and animals that have decomposed over millions of years on the seafloor. Over time, layers of sand and mud settle on top and harden into layers of rock. Heat from Earth's core and the rock overtop turn the organisms into crude oil. Reservoirs are created when the oil sits in the pores of porous rock, such as sandstone.

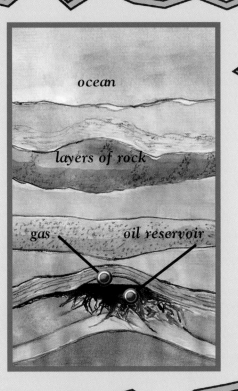

ocean

layers of rock

gas

oil reservoir

The Deepwater Horizon Oil Rig

Before it was destroyed, the Deepwater Horizon was one of the most advanced oil drilling rigs in the world. In 2009, less than a year before the Gulf Oil Spill, the Deepwater Horizon had drilled the world's deepest well at over 35,000 feet (10,668 m) in the Gulf of Mexico. The Deepwater Horizon oil rig burned for almost two days after the disastrous blowout. It sank to the bottom of the ocean on April 22, 2010.

Drilling an Underwater Well

The Deepwater Horizon was a semi-submersible rig that floated on the water. Semi-submersible means that part of it is under water. Semi-submersible oil rigs float on large **buoyancy** tanks. Water is added or removed from the buoyancy tanks to keep the rig afloat. Ocean waters are extremely wavy and rough at times. Computers keep oil rigs steady with a device called the dynamic positioning system, or DP. The DP collects information from different **sensors** aboard the rig. Computers use this information to operate underwater propellers or motors to keep the rig steady—even during stormy weather.

Workers live onboard oil rigs for weeks at a time. Oil rigs have rooms for workers to sleep and relax in when they are not working. There are also kitchens, washrooms, and offices.

The Deepwater Horizon oil rig floated on large buoyancy tanks, as illustrated here.

living quarters for off-duty workers

production platform

An offshore oil rig is also called an exploration rig. It drills a well in the bottom of the ocean to locate oil underneath. After it drills a well, the offshore oil rig moves to drill in another location. An oil platform, sometimes called a production platform, is brought in to extract the oil.

Oil rig workers drill a well.

Exclusive Economic Zone

Every nation owns 200 miles (322 km) from its shorelines into the waters that surround it. This underwater area is called the Exclusive Economic Zone. A United States government agency, called the U.S. Minerals Management Service, leases this underwater land to oil companies such as British Petroleum, also known as BP. Oil companies drill wells on the ocean floor to mine oil.

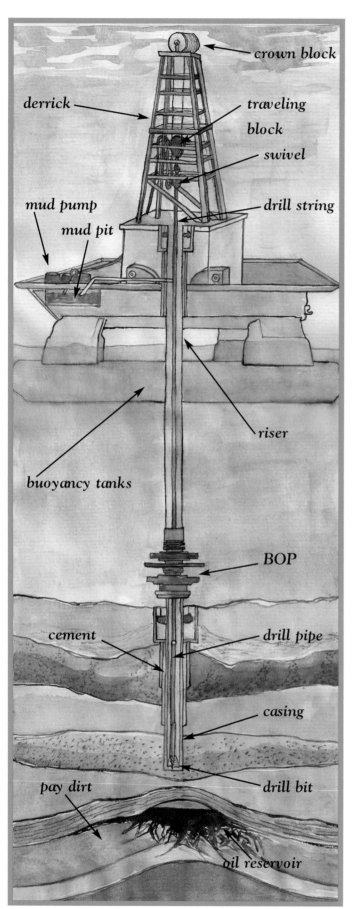

- crown block
- derrick
- traveling block
- swivel
- drill string
- mud pump
- mud pit
- riser
- buoyancy tanks
- BOP
- cement
- drill pipe
- casing
- pay dirt
- drill bit
- oil reservoir

Riser

A large pipe called a riser extends from the oil rig to the seafloor and mouth of the well. The riser protects the equipment used to drill the well from the ocean waters of the Gulf of Mexico.

Inside the riser, a drill string is lowered from the oil rig to the seafloor. A drill string is a number of attached drill pipes that are about 30 feet (nine m) long. As the well is dug deeper, more pipes are attached to extend the length of the drill string.

Drill Bit

A drill bit is attached to the end of a drill pipe. At the mouth opening of the well, the drill bit is around 36 inches (91 cm) in diameter. As the well gets deeper, it becomes narrower. Drill bits used for the final stage of drilling narrow to just under nine inches (23 cm). A circular, rotating platform on the oil rig turns the drill bit. Drill bits are made from very hard substances such as industrial diamonds or steel teeth.

Drill bits cut through the rock layers above the oil deposits.

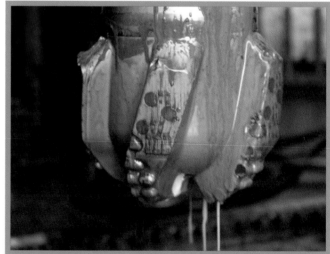

Shown above is a riser on an offshore oil rig.

Drilling Mud

A fluid called drilling mud is stored in the mud pit aboard an oil rig. It is a mixture of water or oil, clay, and chemicals. It is pumped down the drill string and sprayed from nozzles in the drill bit. Drilling mud cools the drill bit. The mud also carries pieces of rock, called cuttings, back to the oil rig. Drilling mud controls the pressure inside the well and keeps the oil from traveling upward.

Pay Dirt

The drill bit digs down until pay dirt is reached. Pay dirt is the layer of Earth that contains the reservoir of oil. Cement is forced down in the space between the drill string casing and the well's rock wall. Cement seals the well and prevents natural gas from escaping and traveling up the well.

Under Pressure

Oil and natural gas are much lighter than the layers of rock and water that sit on top. This creates high pressure in oil and gas reservoirs. When a hole is drilled into a reservoir the pressurized oil and natural gas push upward toward Earth's surface. Oil rigs have methods to control underground oil wells from gushing upward quickly.

Oil wells have a safety device called a blowout preventer (BOP). During offshore drilling, the BOP sits at the head of a well on the seafloor. A blowout preventer is over 50 feet (15 m) tall. It is a stack of valves that seal the drill pipe to prevent a surge of oil or gas, called a kick, coming up from the well. A BOP's final defense is the blind shear ram. This device has steel blades that cut through the well pipe and seal it off at the mouth of the well.

A blowout preventer contains a set of high-pressure valves that prevent a blowout.

Blowout!

The Deepwater Horizon oil rig was drilling in about one mile (5,200 feet or 1,600 m) of water at the Macondo Prospect site. The rig was stationed about 40 miles (64 km) from the Louisiana shore. The oil rig dug over two and a half miles (13,200 feet or 4,000 m) below the seafloor before reaching pay dirt. The well was almost completed when the blowout occurred.

What is a blowout?
A blowout is an explosion of natural gas and oil that rushes from an underground well to the surface. It is sometimes called an oil gusher. Oil and natural gas are highly flammable substances that burn easily. When a blowout occurs oil and gas can easily catch on fire from sparks made by machinery operating on the oil rig.

Attempts are made to put out the fire on the Deepwater Horizon oil rig during the blowout.

Deepwater Horizon's Blowout!

The blowout on the Deepwater Horizon happened at 9:47 p.m. on April 20, 2010. A pocket of gas under pressure escaped from the well and shot straight up to the Deepwater Horizon on the surface of the water. The gas was ignited by sparks from machinery and exploded.

At the time of the disaster, 126 crew members were aboard the Deepwater Horizon. The explosion killed 11 workers and injured 17 others. The BOP failed to cut the well off and seal it. Oil from the unsealed well poured into the Gulf of Mexico.

Oil floats on the water surface in the Gulf of Mexico.

Making the Rules

Oil companies, such as BP, must follow rules and regulations that help prevent blowouts and spills. A government agency called the U.S. Department of the Interior's Minerals Management Service (MMS) makes the safety regulations that oil companies drilling in the country must follow. After the Gulf Oil Spill, the government agency was reorganized and renamed the Bureau of Ocean Energy Management, Regulation, and Enforcement.

A Rush Job

The Deepwater Horizon had successfully dug underwater oil wells for over eight years. But this time the crew was in a hurry. The Macondo well had taken longer than expected. The delay cost BP more than half a million dollars a day. According to the investigators, BP bypassed some safety measures that might have prevented the disaster to get the job done as quickly as possible.

What Happened?

It is difficult to know exactly what happened onboard the Deepwater Horizon during the blowout. Eleven witnesses died during the disaster and important records were lost when the oil rig burned and then sank to the bottom of the Gulf. Investigators believe that the Gulf Oil Spill disaster happened for a number of reasons.

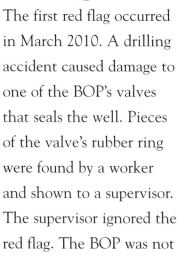

Red Flags

The first red flag occurred in March 2010. A drilling accident caused damage to one of the BOP's valves that seals the well. Pieces of the valve's rubber ring were found by a worker and shown to a supervisor. The supervisor ignored the red flag. The BOP was not checked or repaired.

What is a red flag? A red flag is a warning that something might go wrong.

Once the oil leak was stopped, the damaged blowout preventer from the Deepwater Horizon oil rig was detached from the well and brought to the surface to help with the investigation.

14

Tieback Liner

A tieback liner is often put inside well walls. It is recommended because it blocks gas and oil from flowing up the well. BP decided to use the method of a single pipe surrounded by cement, which is not as safe as a tieback liner. This method takes less time and costs less money to install. BP got permission to use the less safe method from the MMS.

 ## Control pods

Control pods on the BOP receive shutdown signals from the rig to seal off the well in an emergency. Weeks before the blowout, a leak was discovered in one of the control pods. BP was supposed to stop drilling and report the leak to the MMS. It did not do this and continued drilling. The leak was not repaired.

 ## Drilling mud

Drilling mud is supposed to be pumped through the well for a 12-hour period before cement is added. This helps to clean out gas bubbles and cuttings from the well so that the cement can form a safe bond. Drilling mud was pumped through for only 30 minutes.

 ## Centralizers

Rings called centralizers are used to surround the well casing to make sure cement is evenly placed around the casing and the walls of the well. Twenty-one centralizers were recommended for the Macondo well. Only six centralizers were used.

 ## Cement

Independent tests are usually completed to ensure the cement has sealed a new oil well properly. Some tests were performed successfully on the Macondo well. However, additional tests were cancelled.

 ## Lockdown sleeve

A lockdown sleeve is a metal seal that is installed at the mouth of every oil well. The lockdown sleeve had not been installed on the Macondo wellhead when the blowout occurred.

Workers on offshore oil rigs can be put in danger when safety rules are not followed properly.

Stop that Oil!

At the time of the blowout, about 62,000 barrels (almost ten million liters) of oil a day gushed out of the Macondo oil well into the waters of the Gulf of Mexico. As time went on, oil gushing from the well decreased to about 53,000 barrels (over eight million liters) a day.

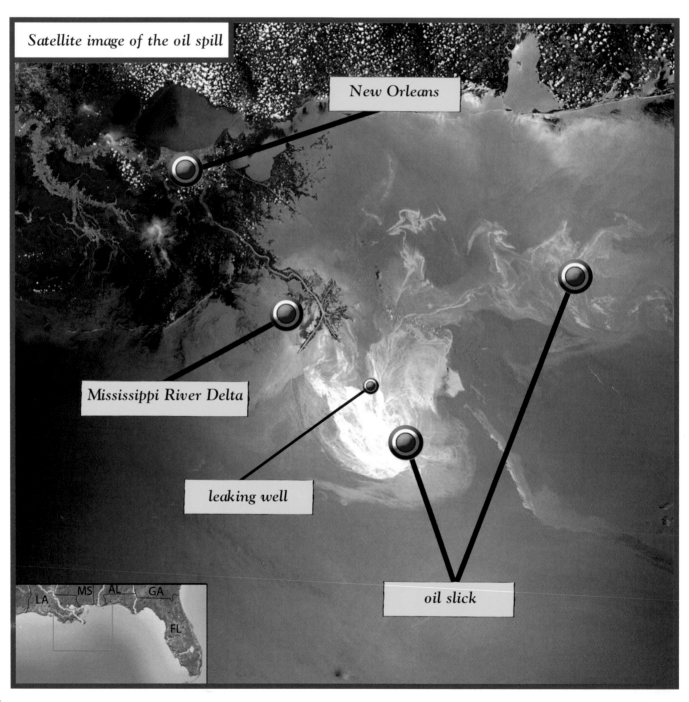

Satellite image of the oil spill

New Orleans

Mississippi River Delta

leaking well

oil slick

LA MS AL GA

FL

Underwater Robots

BP tried to stop the flow of oil by using remote controlled submarines called Remotely Operated Underwater Vehicles, or ROVs. These underwater robots are operated by a person onboard a ship. ROVs are attached to the ship with cables that carry power, lights, and a video camera. The lights and video camera are needed so that the operator can see in the dark ocean depths. The ROVs tried to close the BOP valves and stop the flow of oil from the well. They did not succeed. Oil continued to pour into the Gulf.

Top Hat Containment Dome

A 40-foot (12-meter) steel containment dome was built to help capture some of the oil gushing from the well. A containment dome is a large, hollow structure that resembles a top hat. It works much like an upside-down funnel. The 98-ton (89-metric-ton) dome was placed over a leaking pipe in the hope that leaking oil could be captured and sent through a pipe to a ship on the surface above. The opening of the containment dome was plugged by crystals formed by leaking gas and cold water and the operation was not successful.

(above) ROVs, or Remotely Operated Vehicles, were lowered to the well site to observe the flow of the oil and help stop the leak.

(below) Booms were placed around the shoreline and islands to protect them from oil slicks.

Still Flowing

Oil continued to pour into the Gulf of Mexico from the Macondo well site. A six-inch (15 cm) riser tube was placed inside the leaking pipe to collect some of the oil in a ship above. The tube collected some of the leaking oil and gas but not all of it. The Macondo oil well had to be closed, or capped, permanently.

Top Kill

One month after the blowout, BP tried another idea called top kill, to close the leaking oil well. Top kill involved pumping heavy drilling mud and "junk shot" from a ship on the surface of the water into the BOP to stop the flowing oil. The junk shot was a mixture of rubber tires, golf balls, and rope. The leak was not stopped with top kill.

Try, Try Again

BP tried other containment domes, or top hats, to try to capture some of the oil flowing from the Macondo well. Different top hats were installed using ROVs. The third containment dome was called Top Hat No. 10. It was smaller than the first two but it did capture some of the oil.

A mobile offshore drilling unit holds position directly over the damaged Deepwater Horizon blowout preventer as crews work to plug the wellhead using a technique known as top kill.

Sealing Cap

On July 15, 2010—about three months after the blowout—a sealing cap was placed on the well that stopped the flow of oil. The 30-foot (nine m) tall sealing cap weighed over 160,000 pounds (72,600 kg). It was placed on top of the BOP with help from two ships and underwater ROVs. The sealing cap stopped the flow of oil until relief wells and a permanent cement seal could be installed.

(right) The sealing cap is transported to the Macondo well site.

Relief Wells

Containment domes and sealing caps can only temporarily stop the flowing oil. A permanent solution was needed to stop, or kill, the well completely. To do this, two relief wells were being dug on either side of the Macondo well by two semi-submersible oil rigs. The cost of each new well was about $100 million. The wells cut into the Macondo well at the same place but from different sides. Drilling mud was pumped down the new wells to stop the flow of oil from the Macondo well. Cement was pumped down to permanently seal the well.

On September 19, 2010—almost five months after the Deepwater Horizon blowout—the Macondo well was completely sealed, tested, and officially declared "dead" by the U.S. government.

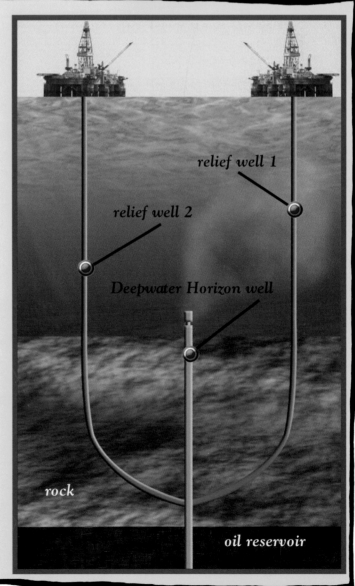

relief well 1

relief well 2

Deepwater Horizon well

rock

oil reservoir

Cleaning Up the Oil

Oil spills in water are one of the most serious and harmful types of environmental disasters. Damage to the environment depends on the type and amount of oil spilled. The Macondo well leaked almost five million barrels of oil into the Gulf of Mexico before it was permanently sealed. Many worked to clean up the oil from the water and shorelines but not all the oil could be removed.

Oil and Water

It is difficult to clean crude oil from such a large body of saltwater. In calm waters, crude oil floats to the top. Oil spreads in a thin layer called an oil slick on top of the water. Often ocean waters, such as the Gulf of Mexico, are very wavy. Waves mix the oil and water into a bubbly brown-looking substance called "chocolate mousse" that is very hard to clean up. Some of the crude oil floated underwater at depths of about 3,000 feet (914 m) in large **plumes**. Some of the oil sank to the bottom and coated coral reefs and other seafloor plant life.

Containment

Oil is contained, or held in one place, by large containment booms. Containment booms float on the water and surround an oil slick. They are filled with plastic foam or air to help them float on water. A nylon skirt hangs down from the floats. It is weighed down in the water with steel chains or lead weights. This skirt helps to gather and contain the oil.

Booms are often attached to one or more boats or ships in the water. Sometimes they are anchored in the water to capture oil passing in water currents. Some booms are made of fireproof materials.

Absorbent booms are used near shorelines. They act like sponges and are used to soak up the oil.

Weathering

Weathering is nature's way of helping clean up an oil spill. Weathering consists of sun, waves, water currents, and weather events. All these things move, and help break down, crude oil. Warm temperatures can make some of the crude oil evaporate into the air. Weathering changes oil into tar balls or mousse. It can also cause oil to sink to the seafloor, or push it to places such as shorelines.

Skimming

Oil is often gathered with a boom so that ships called skimmers can remove the oil from the surface of the water. A skimmer is a boat equipped to bring in the oil from the water's surface and store it in containers onboard. Different skimmers work in different ways. Some bring in the oil on conveyer belts, others vacuum it up through tubes.

Many professional fishers working in the Gulf of Mexico attached skimming equipment to their fishing boats to help skim some of the oil from the water surface during the disaster.

In Situ Burning

Boats pulling fireproof containment booms collect oil floating on the surface of the water near the site of the spill. When the collected oil is thick enough (about the height of a stack of three pennies) it is set on fire and allowed to burn. This is called *in situ burning*. "In situ" means at the original place. Crews must reach the oil spill quickly to collect the oil before it spreads and mixes with water. Water prevents oil from burning.

(below) In situ burning is a good way to remove a lot of oil quickly. It can only be done in calm weather conditions. Burning oil produces a toxic *black smoke that is harmful to breathe. In situ burning is done far away from populated shorelines.*

Oil-Eating Microbes

Microbes are tiny organisms such as bacteria. They eat oil in small, natural leaks, which have always occurred in the Gulf of Mexico. Oil-eating microbes can eat some of the oil but not all of it.

Chemical Dispersants

Dispersants are chemicals used to break up oil spills from the surface of the water. Dispersants move oil from the surface into the water column, below the water's surface. They break the oil into smaller droplets that can be more easily eaten by microbes. Dispersants prevent the oil from reaching land and save marine animals, such as turtles and seabirds, from being coated.

Planes, helicopters, and boats with spray arms spray chemical dispersants on top of oil slicks.

During the Gulf Oil Spill dispersants such as Corexit were used to break up the oil. Corexit is toxic although it is not known exactly how harmful it is for marine life or the environment. It is harmful to people, and workers applying the chemical must wear special masks and suits.

Dispersants were released underwater for the first time ever at the Macondo leak site. Some scientists believe that this created some very large underwater oil plumes. Oil plumes are large bodies of very small parts of oil that cannot be seen from the surface of the water. One underwater oil plume stretched from the Macondo well site for 22 miles (35 km). Plumes float under water in depths of 3,000 to 4,000 feet (900 to 1,200 m).

These workers are using snares to clean up the oil. At first glance, the snare looks like a series of pom-poms connected to a long rope, but it is really a very useful method to recover oil from water.

Marine Life Disaster

Even though oil was cleaned up from the surface of the Gulf, some still remains under water. For marine animals living in the Gulf of Mexico, the combination of oil, chemical dispersants, and lack of oxygen in the water turned their natural **habitat** into a polluted hazard. Scientists are not sure exactly how long the Gulf Oil Spill will affect living organisms in the Gulf of Mexico. Government agencies such as NOAA (the National Oceanic and Atmospheric Administration) study animals living in the Gulf of Mexico. Information collected by NOAA scientists will help if a similar disaster ever occurs again.

Oil and Water: A Toxic Mix

Crude oil is toxic to marine life. Fish take in oxygen by filtering water through their gills. Water **contaminated** with oil droplets can **suffocate** and kill fish instantly as they breathe in the polluted water. Many fish and underwater plant life near the Macondo oil well died instantly because of the oil spill.

Other fish may eat toxic oil droplets. The oil may poison them but not kill them instantly. Oil in very small amounts may harm a fish's vision, sense of smell, and ability to **reproduce**. Small, poisoned fish may in turn be eaten by larger fish farther up the food web. As a result, many fish could be poisoned by oil.

Marine animals such as dolphins may breathe in or eat oil from the spill. Fumes from the oil can knock them out and cause them to drown.

Marine Food Web

Plankton are small, slow-moving marine organisms that are the basis of the marine food web. Different types of plankton include algae, plant life, **microscopic** animals, and larvae or fish eggs. Small fish and some large marine mammals, such as whales, feed on plankton to survive.

Plankton can die when contaminated with oil. Marine **species** that eat plankton may starve. Oil also coats and kills eggs and larvae, which could spell disaster for future generations of marine species living in the Gulf.

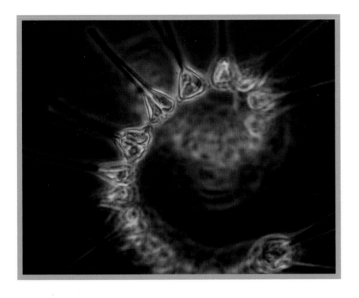

Plankton are the base of the marine food web.

Dead Zones

Oil-eating microbes are plankton that can be both good and bad for the marine environment. They are good because they feast on oil in the water. They produce more and more microbes because the food supply is so great. They are bad for the environment because they also use up a lot of the oxygen in the water. When all the oxygen is used up in a large section of water it becomes hypoxic, or a dead zone. Marine life needs oxygen from the water to survive. Marine life cannot live in a dead zone.

healthy coral

dead coral

When oil-eating microbes use up all the oxygen in the water, coral and other living plant life deep under water can suffocate and die.

Wildlife Disaster

Crude oil in the Gulf waters harmed or killed thousands of birds and animals living there. Some of the oil traveled and spread along shorelines and wildlife habitats. Oil is toxic to all living things. When eaten, oil can poison animals. When coated with oil, animals lose body heat easily, and can drown.

Feathered Friends

Thousands of marine birds such as brown pelicans make the Gulf of Mexico their home. During the oil spill many were killed or harmed. Marine birds have waterproof feathers that help them float on the water and dive for food. Birds floating in oil slicks became covered in oil. When birds' wings are covered in oil, they are unable to fly. Their wings are no longer waterproof, and they can drown. Feathers also keep birds warm. If their feathers become oil-soaked, they cannot mantain heat and the birds can die of hypothermia, or freezing. When birds try to clean the oil from their feathers they swallow some of it. They also eat small fish. If the fish are contaminated by oil, the birds will become contaminated, too. Eating oil can poison the birds and cause liver and kidney damage.

Some wildlife protection agencies, such as the U.S. Fish and Wildlife Service, keep records of how the oil spill affects animals living in the Gulf of Mexico. These records are used to make sure that BP will help restore the wildlife and habitats to their normal state before the disaster occurred.

Other Animals in Danger

Kemp's Ridley turtles are an endangered species of sea turtle that lives in the Gulf of Mexico. The Gulf Oil Spill, and possibly the chemical dispersants used to clean it up, threatens their survival even more. Sea turtles are reptiles that come up to the surface to breathe air. When sea turtles come up for air in an oil slick, the oil can damage their eyes, throats, and lungs. Sea turtles can also be poisoned as they feed off oil-contaminated shellfish and plants. Female sea turtles come ashore to lay their eggs. Oil found in their nesting areas, or on their bodies, can harm or kill their eggs. Newly hatched baby turtles scramble from the beach to the seawater. Beaches and shorelines that are contaminated with oil can poison new baby turtles, too.

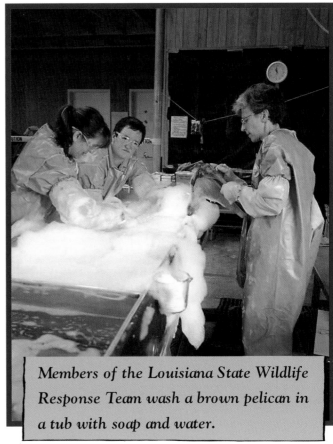

Members of the Louisiana State Wildlife Response Team wash a brown pelican in a tub with soap and water.

The National Oceanic and Atmospheric Administration (NOAA) has rescued over 180 turtles from the Gulf Oil Spill.

Wildlife Rescue

Wildlife rescue workers from groups such as the USFWS (United States Fish and Wildlife Services) and NOAA (the National Oceanic and Atmospheric Administration) search for oiled animals. Some people **volunteer** with agencies, such as the Oiled Wildlife Care Network, to help the animals. Agencies set up telephone hot lines so people can report animals in trouble. Oiled animals that are still alive are carefully examined. They are placed in a warm environment and are given food, water, and antibiotics. They are washed in tubs with soap and water, and rinsed clean. Washing and rinsing can take over an hour for each animal. Afterward they are placed in warm pens to help them dry. When they have fully recovered, they are set free in a clean environment.

Human Disaster

U.S. states surrounding the Gulf of Mexico include Louisiana, Mississippi, Texas, Alabama, and Florida. Many people living near the shorelines of these states were affected by the oil spill disaster. Many who worked in the fishing or tourism industries lost their jobs after the oil spill. Others, especially the workers and volunteers who helped clean up, suffered from health problems.

Commercial Fishing

The Gulf of Mexico is well known for its plentiful seafood industry. Before the Gulf Oil Spill, 20 percent of the United States seafood came from the Gulf of Mexico's waters. U.S. officials closed over 1,000 square miles (2,500 square km) of commercial and recreational fishing areas for many months after the oil spill. Government officials did this to make sure that people would be safe from buying and eating oil-contaminated seafood. Commercial fishing boat owners caught fishing in closed areas were fined up to $140,000 and their boats and fishing gear were taken away from them.

The commercial fishing industry in Louisiana employed over 27,000 people. The industry lost over two billion dollars as a result of the Gulf Oil Spill.

Tourism in the Gulf States

Many tourists are drawn to the Gulf of Mexico's shoreline areas for their clean beaches, water sports, nature watching, and sport fishing. Pollution from the oil spill kept tourists away for many months. Tourism industries, such as hotels and restaurants, suffered **economic** loss. Many people lost their jobs or businesses.

Oil-caked beaches kept tourists away for many months.

Health Risks

It is not exactly known how the Gulf Oil Spill has affected the health of workers who helped clean up after the disaster. Over 45,000 workers were exposed to the oil and chemicals while skimming, burning, or cleaning the beaches of oil. People helping in wildlife clean up were also exposed to these pollutants. The National Institute of Health in the U.S. is doing a study that will help them find out how the oil spill affected people's health.

People living in shoreline communities were affected, too. The Gulf Oil Spill was a disaster that changed many families' lives and livelihoods. Many suffered from stress caused by these changes.

Hired workers clean the oil off the shoreline.

Recovery

No one is sure how long it will take the Gulf of Mexico to recover from this oil spill disaster. Some scientists think it may take more than 30 years. BP, the oil company responsible, has taken financial responsibility for the recovery in the Gulf. The company is working alongside government and volunteer agencies to restore the wildlife, environment, and way of life of people living in the Gulf of Mexico.

Financial Help

Many people and businesses lost money because of the damage of the oil spill. Many of these people filed a claim with the Gulf Coast Claims Facility. BP gave the facility money to **compensate** people who suffered from the oil spill. They have also given money to different state and county governments in the U.S. for damages from the oil spill. At the end of 2010, BP had approved payments of over four billion dollars.

Environmental Recovery

In their efforts to contain and absorb the oil, BP used over three million feet (almost one million meters) of boom. The boom is no longer needed now that the oil well has been capped. BP hired different environmental agencies to help clean and recycle the boom so that it didn't fill up landfill sites. Absorbent boom is drained of its seawater and oil. The seawater is treated and returned to the ocean. The absorbent boom is sent to a plastic recycling facility where it is made into products such as car parts and park benches.

The Obama administration has created a plan to restore the Gulf region's health, environment, and economy.

Vessels of Opportunity

BP began a program called Vessels of Opportunity (VOO) that hired commercial fishers affected by the oil spill. These fishers could not fish because of the oil spill and were not making money to support their families. Instead, BP paid them to use their boats and help clean up the oil from the Gulf.

The VOO program paid commercial fishing vessel owners to help clean up the oil.

Environmental Watchdogs

The U.S. Environmental Protection Agency's (EPA) job is to watch and test air and water quality to see if it is safe. During the Gulf Oil Spill the EPA worked together with the U.S. Coast Guard. They collected samples and tested for oil and chemical pollutants. Agencies such as the U.S. Coast Guard, NOAA, the Food and Drug Administration (FDA), and state and local agencies used the information to help keep people and the environment as safe as possible from the effects of the oil spill. The federal government has put together a plan to restore the Gulf's environment and economy. The plan will be carried out by the Gulf Coast Recovery Council, and paid for by BP.

Glossary

bacteria Single-celled organisms that can only be seen by the human eye through a microscope

blowout An explosion of oil or gas that escapes from an underground well to the surface

buoyancy Having the ability to float

compensate The giving of something to make up for a loss

contaminate To pollute

decompose To rot and break up

domestic Related to or from within a country

economic Of or related to the financial management of what a country produces and sells

extract To remove or take out

habitat An area where animals and plants live

lease A contract that allows the use of an area for a specified amount of money or rent

marine Related to the sea

microscopic Too small to be seen by the human eye but can be seen with the use of a microscope

organisms Any living thing including plants, animals, bacteria, and fungus

plume A stretched out column or band of something

reproduce The act of creating new life

sensors A device that detects and responds to a signal

species A class of organisms having the same characteristics

stress A health condition that occurs when humans or animals are upset by overwhelming or disastrous circumstances and events

suffocate To take away oxygen making it difficult to breathe

toxic Of or relating to a poison that can cause injury or death

valve A device that can stop the flow of a liquid or gas through a hollow tube

volunteer To work or help out for free

Index